A GIFT FOR _____

_____

FROM _____

_____

DATE _____

Published in Nashville, Tennessee, by Thomas Nelson®, Inc.
Thomas Nelson® is a registered trademark of Thomas Nelson, Inc.

Unless otherwise indicated, Scripture quotations are taken from the *New King James Version*.
Copyright © 1979, 1980, 1982, Thomas Nelson, Inc.

Other Scripture quotations are taken from: *New International Version*® (NIV) copyright
© 1973, 1978, 1984 by International Bible Society. Used by permission of Zondervan Publishing House.
All rights reserved.; *New Living Translation* (NLT) copyright © 1996. Used by permission of Tyndale House
Publishers, Inc., Wheaton, Illinois 60189.
All rights reserved.

Project Manager: Lisa Stilwell
Project Editor : Jessica Inman
Art Direction & Design: Linda Bourdeaux, lindamaybe@thedesigndesk.com

ISBN-10: 1-4041-0531-X
ISBN-13: 978-1-4041-0531-7

Printed and bound in China

www.thomasnelson.com

DENISE JACKSON
with Ellen Vaughn

THE
ROAD
HOME

THOMAS NELSON
Since 1798

NASHVILLE   DALLAS   MEXICO CITY   RIO DE JANEIRO   BEIJING

TABLE OF CONTENTS

TABLE OF CONTENTS

INTRODUCTION:
LET GOD TAKE THE WHEEL

I guide you in the way of wisdom
and lead you along straight paths.
When you walk, your steps will not be hampered;
when you run, you will not stumble. —Proverbs 4:11–12 NIV

As it was for so many of us who grew up in the South, church was a big part of my childhood years. I grew up singing hymns and participating in "sword drills"—contests to see who could find a particular Bible passage the fastest. But like so many, as an adult I drifted away from the faith of my childhood. I was married to a country music star, and we had three little girls, and there were plenty of trappings of fame to hold my attention.

Then the storm winds blew into my life, shaking my marriage and my world to their very foundations. It was then that I heard God's whisper, leading me to put my trust in Him, not in myself, not in how I looked, not in my husband, but in Him. Slowly He taught me to put my faith in Him, to let Him steer my life, and soon I found that He had given me brand-new confidence and brand-new joy and restored my marriage. Patiently and lovingly, He led me—and my family—home.

Since then, I've breathed in the wonderful sweetness of my heritage of faith and family. I've also discovered the excitement and joy of growing in God's grace. Every day is a new adventure. I never know where God will lead me next.

No matter where you are in your journey of faith—whether you're just starting out or feeling completely torn apart by circumstances or just need a fresh reminder of God's amazing love—it is my prayer that these simple lessons I've learned along my journey will give you new confidence in God's power to heal and restore anything that's broken. He has a plan for your life. All He needs you to do is let Him take the wheel. ✸

THE
ROAD
of FAITH

WE FIND OUR WAY HOME WHEN WE
TAKE FOOTSTEPS OF FAITH

The LORD knows the days of the upright,
and their inheritance shall be forever. — *Psalm 37:18*

Our lives aren't just random, unconnected collections of scenes without meaning. They have purpose, and as we become more and more tuned in to who God is, we can actually participate with Him in the way our story turns out. We can have peace in the plot's strange twists and turns. We can be free from fear of the bad guys. We can shine with God's love and draw other people to see God's good story in their own lives.

BROKENNESS MOVES MY STORY FORWARD IN A WAY THAT PEACEFUL TIMES DO NOT.

Many of us have chapters that we would prefer had never been written. There are sections of my story that I used to wish I could delete like a computer file. One quick click of the mouse and those chapters would be gone. I just wanted to keep the cheerful parts.

But now I'm beginning to learn that the hard chapters show God's power in a way that the happy ones do not. Brokenness moves my story forward in a way that peaceful times do not. It's in the difficulties that I became desperate to really know God, to cry out to Him.

When everything is going well, we often can't hear God, because the music all around us is turned up too loud. But when the party stops—in those moments of crashing pain, sorrow, and sudden silence—we begin to hear His voice. I've learned that if I listen and lean on His strength, He can help me climb out of the wreckage. As I do, I have new perspectives about what is precious and what is truly important.

> *Trust in the LORD with all your heart,*
> *And lean not on your own understanding;*
> *In all your ways acknowledge Him,*
> *And He shall direct your paths.* — *Proverbs 3:5–6*

For the first fifteen years of my marriage, I was at the wheel of my life's vehicle—let's say it was a white Mustang convertible—and Jesus was in the backseat. Even though in the back of my mind I knew He was there, I didn't think about Him very much, nor did I consider His desires for my life.

Maybe you've been in this situation. You may have accepted Christ as Savior, but that decision hasn't really affected your day-to-day decisions. Or you may believe that God exists, but He seems irrelevant to your everyday experience.

As I became more involved in Bible study and started going back to church regularly, I began to really want to know the One I'd accepted as my Savior back when I was a child. The more I got into the Scriptures, the more I realized that I truly wanted Him to direct my life. So I invited Him to move to the front seat of my life's imaginary car. The passenger seat.

I wanted to be closer to Jesus and to hear what He had to say about the direction I was going. I wanted His input, because I really did believe that His directions would be the best route for me.

But at the same time, I wasn't ready for Him to have complete control. I was going along just fine in my supposed fairy-tale life and was afraid that He might want me to head in an entirely different direction—one that might not be exactly what I had envisioned. I didn't want any bumpy or difficult roads. As long as I was in control, I could listen to Christ but still make my own decisions, just in case He asked me to become a missionary to Africa.

I COULDN'T KEEP THE CAR UNDER CONTROL. I HAD NO IDEA WHICH WAY TO TURN. I WAS TOTALLY LOST, AND I ENDED UP STALLED OUT ON THE SIDE OF THE ROAD.

We rolled along fine with me in the driver's seat. I was happy to have the renewed relationship with Him. I tuned in to radio stations that He liked. I loved the closeness and warmth I felt when He was with me.

But when Alan and I separated, I couldn't keep the car under control. I had no idea which way to turn. I was totally lost, and I ended up stalled out on the side of the road. Finally I begged Christ to get in the driver's seat, to take complete control. I wanted Him to drive my life, no matter where He'd take me.

I FINALLY CRIED OUT, "JESUS, TAKE THE WHEEL!" THIS WAS SCARY, BUT ABSOLUTELY FREEING.

In the words of Carrie Underwood's great song, I cried, "Jesus, take the wheel!"

This was scary, but absolutely freeing. I no longer had to figure out where I was going or how I would get there. In terms of the metaphor, Jesus put the top down, and now the wind blows through my hair. Sometimes we stop and pick up people whose spiritual cars have broken down. It's fun. Life with Jesus in the driver's seat became an open-ended adventure. ✸

*We offer Christ the submission of our hearts,
and the obedience of our lives; and He offers
us His abiding Presence. —Hugh Black*

GOD IS NOT SOME REMOTE,
UNKNOWABLE FORCE.
HE CAN BE FOUND,
KNOWN, AND ENJOYED.
HE OFFERS THE UNIQUE,
FULFILLING RELATIONSHIP
THAT DEEP DOWN, WE ALL LONG FOR.
KNOW THAT HE SEES YOU AND
KNOWS YOUR HEART;
HE KNOWS JUST HOW TO GUIDE
YOU BACK TO HIM.

---

*Let us fix our eyes on Jesus, the author and perfecter
of our faith, who for the joy set before him endured the cross,
scorning its shame, and sat down at the right hand
of the throne of God.* — *Hebrews 12:2* NIV

When Alan left, I was so lost, so full of fear and anger that I could not imagine ever feeling joyful again. I was also full of shame. I felt rejected, exposed, and humiliated by Alan's defection.

Way down deep, I also felt that it was all my fault. I knew that wasn't true. But it's hard for your intellect to win an argument over your feelings, especially when something bad is happening.

My feelings told me that our separation wouldn't have happened if I had just been a little better. Maybe if I had been thinner, smarter, younger, more beautiful, more confident, more fit, funnier, more adventurous, more whatever, then Alan wouldn't have strayed. In my shame, it was all about me—my faults, my deficiencies, ways in which I didn't meet a perfect standard.

Many women struggle with this type of thinking. You don't have to have a celebrity husband to feel such humiliation when he leaves. Shame is an equal-opportunity adversary.

Some of us struggle with it because of traumatic events in our past. Many of us feel shame because of a lifelong feeling that we just don't measure up, and we'll go to any extent of denial to cover it over, because it hurts.

This is where my new relationship with God worked a miracle. As I learned more about Him with my head and experienced His love with my heart, I was absolutely overwhelmed. His love was so big that it crowded out my shame. For a lifetime, I'd tried to be "good enough" . . . good enough to merit my father's love, good enough to make Alan proud, good enough to be considered a "good Christian."

MAYBE IF I HAD BEEN THINNER, SMARTER, YOUNGER, MORE BEAUTIFUL, MORE CONFIDENT, MORE FIT, FUNNIER, MORE ADVENTUROUS, MORE WHATEVER, THEN ALAN WOULDN'T HAVE STRAYED.

Now I knew that I simply couldn't be good enough. What a relief to cheerfully admit my inadequacy! On my own, I could never be in a relationship with a perfect, holy God. But Jesus was good enough. Perfectly good. And because of His death on the cross, in my place, for my sins, God credited Christ's perfect righteousness to my account. My debt was paid in full. Canceled.

So I didn't have to get rid of my shame by the power of positive thinking, like trying to lift a weight that my muscles simply could not budge. No. That weight was lifted from me, freeing me and leaving me lighter than air.

I KNEW I WAS LOVED WITH AN EVERLASTING LOVE SIMPLY BECAUSE OF JESUS.

God's love for me was like a cleansing flood, washing away the sad little rags of shame. I was freed from the need to try to be "good enough" to earn anyone's favor. I knew I was loved with an everlasting love simply because of Jesus. ✹

*What must our natures be like before [God]
can feel at home within us? He asks nothing but a
pure heart and a single mind. He desires but sincerity,
transparency, humility, and love. —A. W. Tozer*

THE GOSPEL TELLS US THE
TRUTH THAT WE ARE SPECIAL AND
SIGNIFICANT SIMPLY BECAUSE WE ARE
CHILDREN OF GOD, NOT BECAUSE
OF HOW WE LOOK OR HOW MANY
GOOD THINGS WE'VE DONE. SO TAKE
COMFORT IN HIS PERFECT LOVE NO
MATTER WHAT STORMS YOU'RE FACING.

*Long ago, even before he made the world, God loved us
and chose us in Christ to be holy and without fault in his eyes.
His unchanging plan has always been to adopt us into his own
family by bringing us to himself through Jesus Christ.*
—Ephesians 1:4–5 NLT

During the early days of our separation, I continued life's normal routines. Mattie and Ali went to school; baby Dani was a wonderful comfort. But my strongest source of support and growth were my relationships with the women in my weekly Bible study.

As I spent time with these women, in church and in our Sunday school class, I was also studying the Bible. Much of it was familiar, as it is to those of us who grew up in a Southern Baptist church. But now the Scripture wasn't just a matter of knowing the right rote answers. It was coming alive for me in a brand-new way. I was beginning to see it as a love story about how God had loved people from the very beginning of time. He had so loved all of us that He actually made a way for our sins to be washed clean and our souls set free, through Jesus. That wasn't just a one-time understanding at age twelve or whenever one walked the aisle to publicly acknowledge one's faith. It was a day-to-day, living reality.

I was also beginning to see that the gospel was all about grace—the undeserved favor we receive from God—not about our performance. It didn't matter how good I'd been or how lovely I looked: God loved me with a wild, intimate, overwhelming love just because He did . . . not because of anything I did. Even as my heart was like a big bruise inside of me because of Alan's leaving, I was beginning to hear the chords of a new song, a song I'd never heard before, a sweet whisper telling me all would be well. ✵

I WAS BEGINNING TO SEE SCRIPTURE AS A LOVE STORY ABOUT HOW GOD HAD LOVED PEOPLE FROM THE VERY BEGINNING OF TIME.

For assuredly, I say to you, whoever says to this mountain, "Be removed and be cast into the sea," and does not doubt in his heart, but believes that those things he says will be done, he will have whatever he says. — *Mark 11:23*

Sometimes on golden fall afternoons I walk down to the huge oak tree that has guarded the river at the edge of our property for more than five hundred years. Around the time Christopher Columbus sailed his wooden ships toward the New World, an acorn the size of a thimble sent a tiny green shoot into the soil we now call ours. Rains came and watered the small sprout.

The sapling grew, sending its roots deeper and deeper into the earth. Its trunk widened over the decades. Centuries passed, and its upper branches reached toward heaven. Wild storms tossed it; the blazing sun scorched it; the raging river flooded its roots. But still the tree stood firm.

Sometimes when I look up at that massive oak, I can't help but think about how Jesus talked about trees. "The kingdom of heaven is like a mustard seed," He said. "Though it is the smallest of all your seeds, yet when it grows, it is the largest of garden plants . . . and becomes a tree, so that the birds of the air come and nest in its branches" (Matthew 13:31–32).

Today, when I stare up at the blue skies above the great tree, I think back to the point in my life when my husband left and the storm winds blew. I wasn't much of a tree; I was more like a twig. I had just begun to put my roots back down in the faith of my youth. I was just beginning to turn my eyes to Jesus, to consider what was really important in life. I had been distracted for many years by the passing pleasures and pressures of this world, but now I was coming home.

I HAD BEEN DISTRACTED FOR MANY YEARS BY THE PASSING PLEASURES AND PRESSURES OF THIS WORLD, BUT NOW I WAS COMING HOME.

Maybe it took Alan's leaving to really rivet my attention on the One who would never leave me. I had only the tiniest mustard seed of faith . . . but in the end God used it to build a stable home for all of us.

For it is God who works in you both to will and to do for His good pleasure. — Philippians 2:13

During the separation, a dear friend counseled me to pray primarily not that Alan would come back, but that God would help me seek Him with all my heart. I knew she was right, and just about half of me was willing to pray that prayer. The other half of me just wanted Alan back. Period.

But I found out a great thing about God. He doesn't wait until our faith or our motives are absolutely pure and perfect. He took my small surrenders, my little steps of willingness, and began to do little miracles with them.

It's like the story of the boy in the New Testament who suffered from epilepsy (Mark 9:17–24). His father brought him to Jesus after many long years of frustration.

Convulsing, the boy foamed at the mouth and rolled on the ground, his arms flailing. His father begged Jesus, "If you can do anything, take pity on us and help us."

"'If you can?'" Jesus repeated. "Everything is possible for him who believes."

"I do believe!" the man shouted in desperation. "Help me overcome my unbelief!" And Jesus healed his son.

I love that story because of the father's raw honesty and Jesus' response to it. So I prayed my own version of the father's words.

"O Lord," I'd say, "I am willing for You to change me. And please help me overcome my unwillingness!"

HE TOOK MY SMALL SURRENDERS, MY LITTLE STEPS OF WILLINGNESS, AND BEGAN TO DO LITTLE MIRACLES WITH THEM.

After a lifetime of trying to be "perfect" in so many ways, suffering from the "disease to please," I found it healing to realize that I didn't have to have perfect faith! I could admit my insufficiency and ask God for what I needed. And I was beginning to believe that He would give it to me. ✺

He satisfies the longing soul,
And fills the hungry soul with goodness.
— *Psalm 107:9*

I began praying one day, stiffly at first, and then more passionately, that God would give me the desire to change. I prayed that He would shape me into the unique person He had created me to be. I desperately wanted Alan back, of course. And part of me was constantly trying to figure out how to fix our marriage, fix myself, control the whole thing, and make Alan return.

Meanwhile, my friends were praying. And I, with a faltering heart but a little shred of faith, was praying that God would give me the will to want His will. No matter what.

One routine morning I dropped the girls off at school, blew kisses, and waved good-bye, and suddenly began talking out loud to God.

"Okay, Lord," I cried. "I am so tired! I can't manage this situation. I can't control what happens or doesn't happen in my marriage. I can't make Alan come back."

In that moment, I totally turned my eyes toward Jesus. "I give up!" I sobbed. "I give in! I know You'll take care of me; I am letting go of it all, and You'll just have to get me through."

IT WAS AS IF THERE WERE A CONNECTION BETWEEN HEAVEN AND EARTH IN THAT OTHERWISE ORDINARY MOMENT. I HEARD GOD'S VOICE. I FELT HIS LOVE.

It was the first time in my life that I had completely let go of my will. I relinquished my desires. My need to try to cling to Alan at all costs. I totally let go and gave it all to God.

And for the first time, I had a tiny, sure sense of real peace. Peace . . . in spite of my circumstances. It was as if there were a connection between heaven and earth in that otherwise ordinary moment. I heard God's voice. I felt His love. And I realized that Alan was never designed to be the center of my life. Christ alone could truly be my All-in-All. ✸

*I have held many things in my hands,
and I have lost them all; but whatever I have placed
in God's hands, that I still possess.*
—Corrie Ten Boom

GOD IS WITH YOU
NO MATTER WHAT.
HE IS STRONGER THAN THE
CHALLENGES IN FRONT OF YOU.
YOU CAN TRUST HIM.
EVEN THOUGH YOU CAN'T SEE HOW
YOUR STORY WILL TURN OUT,
KNOW THAT THE END
IS IN HIS HANDS.

Pray without ceasing.
—*1 Thessalonians 5:17*

Prayer is such a mystery. We don't know how it "works," how God hears prayers offered up to Him on our behalf and then changes the course of our lives. All I know is that the invisible, whispered prayers of friends, acquaintances, and even people I'd never met drew me ever closer to the enormous love and power of God. Through prayer, we can have a mysterious unity of spirit, purpose, and communication that exceeds the bonds of friendships that exist solely on the human level.

While Alan and I were working toward reconciliation, I devoured Stormie Omartian's book *The Power of a Praying Wife.* Each chapter gives Scripture verses and prayers that pertain to specific areas of a husband's life. Every night after the girls were asleep, I read those portions of the Bible out loud and followed the guidelines in Stormie's book to pray for Alan.

I'd pray, "God, please protect our marriage from anything that would harm or destroy it. Shield it from our own selfishness and neglect and from unhealthy or dangerous situations. Set us free from past hurts, memories, ties from previous relationships, and unrealistic expectations of one another. Unite us in a bond of friendship, commitment, generosity, and understanding. Please, make our love for each other grow stronger every day!"

WE CAN HAVE A MYSTERIOUS UNITY OF SPIRIT, PURPOSE, AND COMMUNICATION THAT EXCEEDS THE BONDS OF FRIENDSHIPS THAT EXIST SOLELY ON THE HUMAN LEVEL.

I was beginning to realize that heartfelt prayers are incredibly powerful—not just to change other people or circumstances, but to change me. I realized I could talk with God as if I were sharing with one of my closest friends, pouring out my heart. These times of prayer nurtured my growing trust in Him and gave me new faith in what He might do in the future. ✵

And You will seek Me and find Me,
when you search for Me with all your heart.
— Jeremiah 29:13

Psalm 119:111 says, "Your testimonies I have taken as a heritage forever, / For they are the rejoicing of my heart." Before I really got into Bible study, I would have found a statement like that as dry as dust. But in recent years I turned from regarding the Bible as a boring history book, and I started seeing it as an intimate love letter from God to me. The more I got into it, the more it got into me. I found that it was active and alive. It pierced me with its truths, and it had the power to actually change my life.

To change the metaphor, the more I studied God's Word, the more I found hidden treasures that had been there all along, but I hadn't had the eyes to see them before.

Sometimes friends will say, "Well, that's great for you, Denise, but I just don't have any desire at all to study the Bible."

I understand that . . . but what I've found is that when I ask Him,

God gives me the feelings I can't drum up on my own. When I just don't want to read God's Word, I pray for Him to give me that craving. I pray that He'll make me want to seek Him, because when we seek God, we can be sure of finding Him.

WHEN WE SEEK GOD, WE CAN BE SURE OF FINDING HIM.

I've found that the more I dig into the Bible as His love letter to me, the more I develop a passion both for it and for Him. When my heart is cold and unwilling, I ask Him to change it, and incredibly, He does. As my days unfold, I make sure to schedule uninterrupted time to read God's Word and pray. It's a discipline to do so . . . but when I do it, it fulfills my deepest desires. ❈

God's love is a sun that never sets.
It is always, always, at its full noonday glory.
— Arthur John Gossip

GOD PROMISES
THAT WHEN WE SEEK HIM,
WE WILL FIND HIM,
AND IT'S EVEN GOD
WHO STIRS OUR HEARTS
TO SEEK HIM.
YOU ARE ON HIS RADAR.
IF YOU TURN YOUR HEART
TOWARD HIM,
YOU WILL EXPERIENCE HIM
IN A LIFE-CHANGING WAY.

Morning by morning he wakens me and opens my understanding to his will. The Sovereign LORD has spoken to me, and I have listened. — Isaiah 50:4–5 NLT

Like many Christians, I had wanted a more vibrant prayer life for years. Though I'd been committed to regular Bible study for several years, my prayers were sporadic and often dull or cold. I know I'm not alone in this—lots of Christians feel that their prayer lives aren't quite what they could be.

In my own journey with Jesus, a specific set of tools has revolutionized my prayer life. A friend gave me a book by Becky Tirabassi titled— appropriately—*Let Prayer Change Your Life*. In it Becky describes her own struggles with having a regular and invigorating prayer time, and how God gave her some specific, practical steps that changed it—and her—dramatically. As I engaged in these steps, prayer became an entirely new adventure for me.

I start with reading God's Word, using a Bible reading program developed by Becky that includes readings for each day of the year. After slowly reading the Scriptures, I open my mind and heart to what the Holy Spirit might be saying to me. Then I get out my prayer journal. It has neat, organized sections in which to jot my prayers.

- In the praise section, I often rewrite prayers from the Psalms in my own words in order to give God the glory that He deserves.

- Next I admit my sins to God, jotting down whatever He brings to mind and asking His forgiveness so my relationship with Him can be current, without any old baggage or garbage between us.

- In the request section, I write down my concerns and requests for myself and others. It has been incredibly rewarding to look back at these journal pages and see all the prayers that God has answered. Some answers have been those I asked for; others have been way outside the box of my own expectations.

- The next section is for giving thanks to God. The more I write on these pages, the more comes to mind. Gratitude to God perpetuates more gratitude. It's addictive!

- In the listening section, I write whatever I feel the Holy Spirit is saying to me. It might be a certain Scripture that I read that day or perhaps a new sense of God's guidance in a particular situation. Or something may come to mind that I feel the Lord is leading me to do that day.

- Lastly, I write down anything from the Scripture readings that I want to memorize or apply in a particular way.

THE MORE WE SEEK HIM OUT, THE MORE WE'RE AT PEACE AS WE SEE HIS DIRECTION IN OUR LIVES.

My grandmother had her own disciplines for spending time with God in prayer; my daughters may well have different ways that they do it. But for me, this system has been enormously helpful. What is important is not the particular format, but the priority of time reserved for connecting with God. The more we seek Him out, the more we're drawn to be like Him—and the more we're at peace as we see His direction in our lives. ✹

*The Bible is a letter from God
with our personal address on it.*
—Søren Kierkegaard

BIBLE READING AND PRAYER
ARE THE WAYS TO REALLY
CONNECT WITH JESUS
AND DEVELOP STRONG FAITH.
IT'S NOT OUR STRENGTH;
WE GRAFT OURSELVES INTO
HIS STRENGTH AND,
LIKE THE BRANCHES OF A TREE,
DRAW LIFE FROM THE VITALITY
OF THE TRUNK AND ROOTS.

He who heeds the word wisely will find good,
And whoever trusts in the LORD, happy is he.
— Proverbs 16:20

On the morning of September 11, 2001, Alan was at home in his study. I was at my Tuesday morning Bible study. The children were at school. When I heard the news, I rushed home, and like everyone else in the country, Alan and I stood in front of the television, our hands over our mouths, tears in our eyes.

A few weeks after that terrible day, Alan woke in the middle of the night. The melody and a few lines of a song were running through his mind. He crept downstairs to his office and sang into his little handheld voice recorder, worried that if he waited until morning, he'd forget it all. Then he came upstairs and quietly slipped back into bed, not realizing that what he had just recorded would touch so many who were suffering from the 9/11 tragedies.

The next morning he finished writing the song. It was called "Where Were You (When the World Stopped Turning)," and it eventually went to the top of not just the country charts, but the general market and pop genres as well. It struck a chord.

In some ways Alan is a very complicated person. In other ways, as his song says, he's just a singer of simple songs. His simplicity nailed what many people felt about September 11. It touched many for whom the attacks were not only a horrible catastrophe, but also a wake-up call about what really matters in this life.

ALAN AND I STOOD IN FRONT OF THE TELEVISION, OUR HANDS OVER OUR MOUTHS, TEARS IN OUR EYES.

The terrorist assaults pierced the hearts of people across America and around the world. They brought everything to a halt for a while. They sifted out unessential things that so often clamor for our attention. They highlighted what was truly important. ✷

Surely I am with you always, to the very end of the age.
— Matthew 28:20 NIV

I once heard a story about an elderly lady who went to her young pastor to plan her funeral arrangements. She listed her choice of hymns, Scripture selections, and exactly what outfit she wanted to wear in her open casket. And then she said, "There's one more thing. I want you to make sure the funeral home takes care of one final arrangement. I want them to put me in my casket with a silver fork in my hand."

"A fork?" the pastor repeated.

"Yes, a sterling silver dessert fork. And when everyone comes and looks in the casket to pay their respects, and they say, 'Why in the world does she have a dessert fork in her hand?' I want you to tell them the reason why."

"And what might that reason be?" the pastor asked, scratching his head.

The elderly woman smiled. "Son, when I was young, my parents told me to eat up my dinner because the best part of the meal was yet to come. We always looked forward to dessert, knowing it would be sweet. So I want you to tell those people that I was buried with a dessert fork in my hand because I know that after this life comes the sweetest part of all. Tell them I know that, by God's grace, the best is yet to come!"

I don't think I want to be buried with a dessert fork in my hand, but I agree with the lady in this story. I've learned that all kinds of troubles will come in this life. Jesus said to expect them. They're not the exception; they're the norm.

I DON'T HAVE TO BE AFRAID OR ANXIOUS WHEN THE CRISES COME. GOD IS WITH ME.

But I'm learning that I don't have to be afraid or anxious when the crises come. God is with me. He will give me whatever I need to get through life's challenges. He can do miracles in me, right in the midst of troubled times. ✹

May He grant you according to your heart's desire,
and fulfill all your purpose. — Psalm 20:4

Nine years ago the Lord gave me the unlikely desire to write a book. At first, it seemed absurd even to consider it. I had no idea how to begin, no idea how to accomplish it, no idea of the steps to take to make it happen. I'm not a writer, and I'm also just about the last person in the world who would want to open up her life for others to read. I don't like to be exposed.

I'M BEGINNING TO LEARN THAT WITH GOD, NOTHING IS IMPOSSIBLE. I'M STARTING TO DREAM BIGGER DREAMS.

But God gave me this crazy idea that wouldn't go away, the idea to write about what God had done in my life. I felt that other people might relate to parts of my story and that maybe God could use it to draw others to Himself, so they could enjoy His love and freedom too. And eventually, in God's timing, He put together the team to create the book, so I didn't have to go it alone.

Writing a book may not seem like a big deal to someone else. But in this case and in so many others, I'm beginning to learn that with God, nothing is impossible. I'm starting to dream bigger dreams, knowing that, as Paul declared in Philippians 4:13, I can do everything through Christ who gives me strength. ✳

It is not what we do that matters, but what a sovereign God chooses to do through us. —Charles Colson

WHEN WE TURN EVERYTHING
OVER TO GOD, HE DOES FOR US
WHAT WE CAN'T DO FOR OURSELVES.
HE HAS GREATER STRENGTH
THAN WE COULD EVER HAVE ON OUR OWN,
AND WHEN WE TRUST IN HIM,
HE UNFAILINGLY SHOWS
HIMSELF FAITHFUL.

THE
ROAD
of HOPE

WE FIND OUR WAY HOME WHEN WE
WALK WITH A SENSE OF HOPE

But seek first the kingdom of God and His righteousness,
and all these things shall be added unto you.
— Matthew 6:33

Recently I met a woman who asked if she could take pictures of our estate. She was a Sunday school teacher, and she'd been telling the kids in her class about how Jesus said that He was preparing mansions in heaven for them. Since these kids had never laid eyes on a mansion, she wanted them to see pictures of one so they could better visualize the wonderful splendor of Jesus' promise.

I'm grateful for our beautiful home. Every time Alan and I drive into its big gates, we're floored that we actually get to live in such an incredible place. But it's made of bricks and mortar, and it will one day crumble. Christ's heavenly mansions will be more beautiful than we can imagine, and they will last forever. And they're available not just for the select few who make it big in this world, but for all who look to Jesus.

I've learned through a lot of tears, over a lot of time, that possessions alone will never satisfy the hunger we all have inside. The only thing that can fill us up to overflowing is a real relationship with Jesus. That's not just nice religious talk. It's true. While material stuff is great fun, and I enjoy it and I try to share whatever I have, I could give it all up tomorrow. But I could never give up Jesus—and, more importantly, He will never give up on me.

THE ONLY THING THAT CAN FILL US UP TO OVER-FLOWING IS A REAL RELATIONSHIP WITH JESUS.

Softly and tenderly, He calls each of us, His arms flung wide to hold us tight. He can give us real joy, true peace, and fulfillment forever. This isn't about religion or going to church or looking holy or trying to do all the right things. This is about being in an unbreakable bond with Jesus, living with Him in a cherished connection of love. He longs to bless us abundantly, beyond our wildest dreams. ❈

*And we know that all things work together for good
to those who love God, to those who are called
according to His purpose. — Romans 8:28*

When I was pregnant with our third child, Dani, I had an ultrasound at my eleven-week checkup. Alan was with me, and he noticed that there were two "peanut shapes" inside me. He asked the nurse if there were two babies, but she didn't really answer.

"I'll get the doctor to take a look," she said. When the doctor looked at the screen, he confirmed that there were indeed two babies . . . but one was not viable. "This is what we call a 'disappearing twin,'" he said gently. "It happens every once in a while."

For whatever reason, the little fetus had stopped growing. While Dani's heart was beating strong, her twin's heart had gone still. His tissue would eventually break down and be absorbed into the uterine lining.

The joy of celebrating one baby, and the grief of losing another, seemed to foreshadow the extreme roller coaster of emotions that my heart would experience in the coming months. I often thought sadly of the twin who disappeared. Would Dani have had a twin brother like I had? I didn't know why he didn't grow. Sometimes I wondered if having twins during this period of terrible stress would have been too much for me to handle. Only God knows.

I CAN CHOOSE TO BELIEVE THAT HE IS GOOD, AND IN CONTROL, AND TO TRUST HIM . . . OR I CAN TRY TO CONTROL MY OWN LIFE.

But the mystery of it all reminded me that God is far greater than I can imagine. I can't understand His ways. In sorrow and loss as well as in joy, I always have a choice to make. I can choose to believe that He is good, and in control, and to trust Him . . . or I can try to manipulate every outcome and rigidly try to control my own life. During the sad time of separation from Alan, it became clearer and clearer to me that I couldn't say that I trusted God to be in charge of my life and then grab back the steering wheel whenever I didn't understand what He was doing. I had to hold on to His promises and all the ways He'd proven Himself faithful; and I had to choose to put my hope in Him. ❈

We do not understand the intricate pattern
of the stars in their courses, but we know that
He who created them does, and that just as surely
as He guides them, He is charting a safe course for us.
— Billy Graham

WHEN IT'S ALL ABOUT HIM,
THEN OUR STORIES NOT ONLY
HAVE AN UNBELIEVABLY
HAPPY ULTIMATE ENDING,
BUT EVERY CHAPTER OF LIFE
—HAPPY OR SAD—
IS SOMEHOW SWEETER
THAN THE ONE BEFORE.
DURING THOSE SAD CHAPTERS,
REMEMBER HIS STRENGTH
AND HIS LOVE FOR YOU,
AND TAKE COURAGE.

The joy of the LORD is your strength.
— Nehemiah 8:10

After he asked me out on a second first date, Alan and I had gone through lots of counseling, and then we continued to "date," strange as that was. We had laid out our relationship on the table, and the counselors had analyzed it all, like doctors probing a big pile of intestines or something. Now it was time to put some of that analysis into action. We were moving from the theoretical to the practical. We knew what was wrong with our old patterns; all we had to do was create new, healthy habits of interacting with each other.

Easier said than done.

One of the biggest areas for me had to do with my own self-confidence and comfort in my own skin. I had lots of old tapes playing in my head, tapes with destructive themes like "I'm not good enough" . . . "I'm not Alan's soul mate" . . . "I'll never be the right one for him" . . . "I'm so dependent, I could never make it without Alan."

These bad tapes had to be ejected, thrown away, and replaced with new themes that I downloaded from my relationship with God. Through the words of Scripture, He told me, "Denise, I've loved you with an everlasting love, and I will build you up" . . . "I have great plans for you, and I am doing a new thing to give you new freedoms in your marriage" . . . "My grace is sufficient for you—you have everything you need to make it, for I am strong when you are weak, and I am with you always!"

THROUGH THE WORDS OF SCRIPTURE, HE TOLD ME, "DENISE, I'VE LOVED YOU WITH AN EVERLASTING LOVE, AND I WILL BUILD YOU UP."

Whatever you're going through, replacing old tapes with God's Word is so important. That's where you'll find your strength, the strength to move forward into a new era in your life. ❋

Delight yourself also in the LORD,
And He shall give you the desires of your heart.
— Psalm 37:4

After we spent months in counseling and working on new habits and patterns in our relationship, something happened, something so many people had prayed long and hard for: Alan moved back into our home one May day. Tears welled up in my eyes as he told the children that he was here to stay.

GOD WAS CALLING US BACK TO OUR MARRIAGE VOWS, AND HE WAS GIVING US A FRESH START.

"Girls, I want you to know something," he said. "Fifty years from now, when you are grown and have families of your own, your mama and I will still be together. You don't need to worry. We'll be right here, sitting in rocking chairs on the front porch together." I knew that nothing could have made the girls happier than hearing those words.

The following Sunday was Mother's Day. The girls and I went

to church, and when we returned home, the house was full of the aromas of roast beef, mashed potatoes, fresh green beans and corn, buttery yeast rolls, and warm banana pudding. Alan ushered us into the dining room. He had set the table with our best china and crystal, linen napkins, white candles, and an enormous floral arrangement.

"Happy Mother's Day!" he shouted.

I was overwhelmed. Alan's thoughtfulness in making this day special was just one of the many things he did for me in the weeks and months to come—physical acts of kindness to show me the intentions of his heart. He was putting the past behind and making our marriage the best that it could be.

God was calling us back to our marriage vows, and He was giving us a fresh start.

I'm convinced that we wouldn't have had the chance to start over if I hadn't learned to trust God as my All-in-All. He took the broken pieces of our marriage and created something far better than before.

No good thing will He withhold
From those who walk uprightly. — *Psalm 84:11*

Once it seemed as if our marriage actually might last, I told Alan that I wanted visible reminders of the new commitment that was written in our hearts. "We've had a fresh start," I said. "I want a ceremony where other people can see us making this new commitment. I want our anniversary to be a day of renewal."

Our marriage was being restored. We believed that, by God's grace, we'd been refined by difficulties, purified, and given the gift of a new, more durable marriage. And to commemorate all this, we had new rings made of platinum. Our new rings were a symbol of the commitment to a deep, true love that had its roots in the healing love and amazing grace of God.

And so, on our anniversary, our family gathered in a small chapel with a few friends. Robert Wolgemuth, my friend and Sunday school teacher, led the ceremony, opening the service with one of my favorite Scripture passages, Jeremiah 29:11–13: "'For I know the plans I have for you,' says the LORD. 'They are plans for good and not for disaster, to give you a future and a hope. In those days when you pray, I will listen. If you look for me in earnest, you will find me'" (NLT).

OUR MARRIAGE WAS BEING RESTORED. OUR LOVE HAD BEEN REFINED BY THE CLEANSING FIRE OF GOD'S LOVE AND FORGIVENESS.

Never before had I so strongly realized the truth of these verses. The Lord had heard my petitions to Him and restored my marriage. He took our brokenness and sinfulness and actually brought good out of it. When I called to Him in desperation, He was faithful to make Himself known to me.

God has a plan for all of us, a plan full of hope. Even when things seem absolutely, irreversibly awful, if we seek Him, He will lead us back home and restore to us even more than what we've lost. ✸

Do not look to your hope,
but to Christ, the source of your hope.
—Charles Haddon Spurgeon

EVEN IF YOU'VE
LOST YOUR WAY, LOST HOPE,
OR LOST EVERYTHING,
YOU'RE NEVER TOO FAR AWAY
FROM GOD FOR HIM TO FIND YOU.
TURN CONTROL OVER TO HIM, AND
YOU'LL SOON DISCOVER
THAT HE IS MORE THAN ABLE
TO WORK MIRACLES
IN YOUR LIFE.

I have seen his ways, and will heal him;
I will also lead him,
and restore comforts to him.
—*Isaiah 57:18*

The older I get, the more clearly I see how the pattern of brokenness and restoration that we so often experience in our lives reflects the big picture of God's great story.

The gospel is all about God coming to earth as a real human being. Jesus walked on dusty roads. He laughed and went on picnics. He felt weakness and pain. In the end, He was tortured and executed. In human myths, people are sacrificed for gods . . . but in Christianity, God gave Himself for His people. And out of that ultimate weakness—that "most significant shattering," as Christian counselor Dan Allender puts it—came the glory of resurrection. Because Christ's story on earth ended in triumph, we have the assurance that ours will end well, too, if we know Him.

God's story is far stronger than the nicest fairy tales we know. As I've seen in my own life, it unfolds over time. He weaves together strands of joy, sorrow, friends' prayers, and His mysterious will.

A few Christmases ago, my friend Bobbie Wolgemuth, who had encouraged me and prayed for me throughout the separation and everything after, flipped on her TV. We'd lost touch with the Wolgemuths after Alan and I had renewed our vows, and she didn't really know how we were doing in terms of our recommitment to God and each other. When she turned on her TV, she happened to flip to a Christmas special on CMT (Country Music Television) featuring Alan and the music of his Christmas CD.

BECAUSE CHRIST'S STORY ON EARTH ENDED IN TRIUMPH, WE HAVE THE ASSURANCE THAT OURS WILL END WELL, TOO, IF WE KNOW HIM.

Wearing a bright red jacket and his trademark Stetson cowboy hat, Alan sang "Santa Claus Is Coming to Town" while Ali and Dani, both dressed in sparkling red elf costumes, danced with a few friends from Ali's dance class. Mattie read the account of the first Christmas from the Gospel of Luke as a guitarist played a beautiful introduction to "Silent Night." The cameras zoomed in on our mothers, who were smiling and clapping with the audience. And at the end of the show, our entire family came onto the stage, put our arms around one another, and sang the sweet words to the Christmas song Alan had written for his album.

Watching the broadcast, Bobbie shook her head in wonder. The words from just one of the many prayers she had prayed for us and written in her prayer journal—four years earlier—popped into her mind.

"I pray that Alan will write songs of victory," she had written back in 1998, "and that You would surround his family with deliverance and Your abiding love. May they rejoice in the Lord and be glad! May they sing with upright hearts!"

BOBBIE COULD SEE THAT GOD WAS CONTINUING TO UNFOLD HIS GREAT STORY IN OUR LIVES.

And there we were, courtesy of Bobbie's TV screen. We weren't perfect, but we were upright, rejoicing in the Lord and being glad. And we were singing with all our hearts. Bobbie could tell that her prayer for us had been answered. She could see that God was continuing to unfold His great story—the story, as Alan's song put it, of "hope and joy and peace"—in our lives. ✷

Never be afraid to trust an unknown future to a known God. —Corrie Ten Boom

WHEN WE FILL OUR MINDS
WITH GRATITUDE FOR THE WAY
GOD HAS REDEEMED OUR PAST,
THE FUTURE SEEMS LIKE
AN UNFOLDING ADVENTURE.
WE GET TO EXPERIENCE
GOD'S GREAT PLAN FOR OUR LIVES
ONE DAY AT A TIME.

For the LORD your God will bless you in all your harvest and in all the work of your hands, and your joy will be complete. — Deuteronomy 16:15 NIV

For years Alan's mother had been asking him to record a gospel album. After years of promising to do it later, Alan finally sat down with an old Baptist hymnbook and chose fifteen classic songs, which he recorded with wonderful but minimal accompaniment and no fancy arrangements. He wanted the old hymns to sound the way he remembered them from church in his childhood.

When Mama Ruth first heard this unique Christmas present, tears rolled down her cheeks. She couldn't help but reflect on everything Alan had been through. She wept as she thought of the long journey he had made to get to this place of wanting to sing those hymns for her, and being able to do so with real conviction in his heart.

We made additional copies of Alan's gospel CD and gave them to extended family and friends. Then, to our surprise, the record label executives decided that our little family CD needed to be released commercially. It was an odd decision. The album wasn't slick or professional. The label wasn't planning to promote it. And they knew that the country radio stations wouldn't play it. In other words, releasing it made no commercial sense. But they did it anyway.

SHE WEPT AS SHE THOUGHT OF THE LONG JOURNEY HE HAD MADE TO GET TO THIS PLACE OF WANTING TO SING THOSE HYMNS.

To everyone's surprise, the *Precious Memories* CD shot up the charts and stayed there. Released in February 2006, it spent twelve of its first nineteen weeks at the top of the country, Christian, and gospel sales charts.

No one in the music world could explain why *Precious Memories* did so well and received so many honors. No one could figure it out at all . . . except maybe Alan's mother. It seems that when God has special plans for something, He will accomplish exactly what He intends—despite the odds against it. ✹

When we come to the end of ourselves,
we come to the beginning of God.
— Billy Graham

WHEN YOU CHOOSE TO LET
JESUS DRIVE YOUR LIFE'S CAR,
REST ASSURED THAT YOU
CAN TRUST HIM.
HE HAS DESTINATIONS IN MIND
YOU NEVER WOULD HAVE BEEN
ABLE TO FIND ON YOUR OWN.
WATCH AND WAIT TO SEE WHAT
WONDERFUL THINGS
HE HAS IN STORE FOR YOU.

For we know that if our earthly house, this tent, is destroyed, we have a building from God, a house not made with hands, eternal in the heavens. —*2 Corinthians 5:1*

One Wednesday afternoon in June, I got a call from my sister Jane. Daddy had fallen and broken his leg. "I think you'd better come to Newnan," she told me.

My father was ninety-one years old. Obviously, I knew that he wasn't going to be with us forever . . . but still, he had come through three major surgeries in the past three years, and I assumed he would come through this medical challenge as well. I didn't realize that the time had come to say good-bye.

I got to Newnan the following morning. Daddy was sedated and dozing in intensive care. My mother and sister were in the room with him, and my mama's face was weary with worry.

I pulled the hard hospital chair close to his narrow bed. I sat with him for hours, holding his hand, and watching his chest rise and fall with each shallow breath. He dozed on and off throughout the afternoon. Then he mumbled to me through the oxygen mask that covered his nose and mouth.

"Nisey," he whispered, "do you know what Jesus said to Peter and Andrew?"

I was surprised. Daddy knew the Bible, but we had never spent a lot of time sitting around discussing the New Testament.

"Why, yes," I said slowly. "I remember. Jesus told Peter and Andrew to follow Him and that He would make them fishers of men. And so they left their nets and followed Him."

I ASSUMED HE WOULD COME THROUGH THIS MEDICAL CHALLENGE AS WELL. I DIDN'T REALIZE THAT THE TIME HAD COME TO SAY GOOD-BYE.

"That's right," he said, smiling. "Fishers of men."

Those were the last words my father said to me. Hospice nurses say that dying people often speak in metaphors to signal to the living that they're about to pass on, and I realized from my dad's words that death wasn't threatening to him. A lifelong fisherman, he was simply preparing for his journey across the last great river, smiling at Jesus, and thinking about fishing for men. Knowing this was a great comfort to me.

I SMILED AS I WATCHED MY MOTHER PUT THE SOFT FABRIC UP TO HER FACE, TEARS IN HER EYES, AND BREATHE IN THE FAINT SCENT OF MY FATHER.

The next day, as dawn broke and a new day began, my father slipped away. I imagined him talking with Peter and Andrew firsthand, swapping fishing stories.

An ending . . . and a new beginning.

The next Christmas my mother came to visit with us. As she opened my present to her—a quilt made of scraps of my daddy's old shirts—Alan's CD of hymns happened to be playing "When We All Get to Heaven." I smiled as I watched my mother put the soft fabric up to her face, tears in her eyes, and breathe in the faint scent of my father as the music played:

When we all get to heaven,
What a day of rejoicing that will be!

When we all see Jesus,
We'll sing and shout the victory!

It was a moment of hope, the greatest hope of all: the hope of a conquered death. Because of Jesus, I knew my family could look forward to a reunion in heaven. We will see Jesus, and what a day of rejoicing that will be. ✳

Christ made no promise that those who followed Him . . .
would enjoy a special immunity from pain and sorrow—
nor did He Himself experience such immunity.
He did, however, promise enough joy and courage,
enough love and confidence in God
to enable those who went His way
to do far more than survive.
—J. B. Phillips

GOD OFFERS US A HOPE
THAT DEFIES DEATH, SICKNESS,
AND THE WORST OF CIRCUMSTANCES.
WHEN WE HOPE IN HIM, WE KNOW
THAT ALL OUR TRIALS ARE TEMPORARY
AND THAT HE STANDS BESIDE
US IN THE MIDST OF THEM ALL.

For You, O God, have heard my vows;
You have given me the heritage of those
who fear Your name. — Psalm 61:5

As I reflected on my origins in those sweet-sad days after my father's death, I knew that I had deep spiritual roots. I remembered Mama Jack, my daddy's mother. She had a well-worn black leather Bible, and even in her nineties, she read through it again and again without needing glasses. Looking back now, I could see that some of the blessings I was receiving, even in the aftermath of my father's death, were because of my grandmother's faith.

Her prayers had shaped me. I had a legacy of faith as sweet as the old hymns that we sang at family reunions, as dear as my mother's soprano soaring over my father's funeral. That legacy was stronger than the forces that had shaken me over the years, and it was a heritage I could pass on to my children.

What Mama Jack had prayed for her descendants was creating a legacy of faith that would be passed to future generations. I thought about Mama Jack's sweet, devout spirit . . . and I purposed to spend more time sinking my roots down into the Bible that she had so treasured.

Throughout the day, I "turn my eyes upon Jesus" by reading the Bible, listening to sermons or uplifting music, and connecting with friends who share the same passion. The more I focus on Jesus, the more I can be filled up with His love and the more I can pass that love on to others . . . to my family, friends in need, whomever.

WHAT MAMA JACK HAD PRAYED FOR HER DESCENDANTS WAS CREATING A LEGACY OF FAITH THAT WOULD BE PASSED TO FUTURE GENERATIONS.

That's how it was with my grandmother's love for God's Word. When I was younger, I respected her faith, but I didn't really understand it. Now I feel as if I've gotten a taste of the great secret she knew, and it makes me hungry for more. And I pray that I might instill that same love for God and His Word in my own children and grandchildren.

But we all, with unveiled face, beholding as in a mirror
the glory of the Lord, are being transformed into the same image
from glory to glory, just as by the Spirit of the Lord.
—2 Corinthians 3:18

I would love to say that after Alan and I renewed our vows, we were instantly changed into perfect Christians and the perfect couple. It would be great if life were like those extreme-makeover TV shows, where people are rejuvenated into ideal versions of themselves, into what they've always wanted to be.

WE KNOW OUR PROGRESS WILL BE SLOW . . .
BUT WE'RE MOVING IN THE RIGHT DIRECTION.

But lasting transformation takes a lot longer than an hour-long TV show or the amount of time it takes for plastic surgery to heal. Growth in human relationships takes time. In our committed-but-not-perfect marriage, Alan and I get up every morning and take each day as it comes, with a renewed pledge to each other and to Christ. We know our progress will be slow . . . but we're moving in the right direction.

I've come to realize that life's journey isn't a quick transformational spin, but a long, hard trek of slow growth in an upward direction. Spiritually speaking, sanctification—or becoming more like Jesus—is a lifelong process. We can't get bogged down in discouragement when we feel as if we're not where we should be. We have to trust that God has us in a place of growth and that "He who has begun a good work in you will complete it until the day of Jesus Christ" (Philippians 1:6).

God is to us like the sky to a small bird,
which cannot see its outer limits and cannot reach
its distant horizons, but can only lose itself in the greatness
and immensity of the blueness. — John Powell

WHEN WE SPEND TIME
GETTING TO KNOW GOD,
WE DISCOVER WHO HE IS AND
WHAT HE WANTS FOR OUR LIVES—AND
HIS PLANS ARE FAR BETTER THAN
ANY WE COULD DREAM UP
FOR OURSELVES.

THE
ROAD
of LOVE

WE FIND OUR WAY HOME WHEN WE LET
LOVE GUIDE OUR STEPS—EVEN
WHEN THE PATH IS DARK

_Think of ways to encourage one another to outbursts of love
and good deeds. And let us not neglect our meeting together,
as some people do, but encourage and warn each other,
especially now that the day of his coming back again
is drawing near._ —Hebrews 10:24–25 NLT

In the fall of 1995, Mattie started kindergarten at a private school in Nashville. I was glad to connect with other women who had children Mattie's age. One of them, Jane Smith, sent out an invitation to all the moms of the lower-school students, inviting us to be part of a prayer group in her home. I thought that being a part of this group would be a great way to make new friends, so I joined.

Not only did I form some great, long-lasting friendships, but my time spent with these women was the beginning of my real spiritual growth. We studied Christian parenting books. We confided our concerns for each of our children and prayed for God's blessings and protection for them.

Since I hadn't yet found a home church, Jane invited me to visit hers, and we started attending regularly. Mattie had school friends in her Sunday school class, so she enjoyed it. I also found a Sunday school class with a very gifted teacher, Robert Wolgemuth. I was drawn to the Scripture like never before. For the first time in my life, the Bible came alive for me. It was relevant. Personal. True. I began to look forward to Sunday mornings. The gospel was presented in a way that I could apply it to my everyday life. Finally, my spiritual life was beginning to get back on track. All because a mom sent out an invitation to join together in prayer.

NOT ONLY DID I FORM SOME GREAT, LONG-LASTING FRIENDSHIPS, BUT MY TIME SPENT WITH THESE WOMEN WAS THE BEGINNING OF MY REAL SPIRITUAL GROWTH.

Reflecting on this now, I realize again that none of us can make it in life on our own. We need one another for encouragement and comfort and spiritual growth. By reaching out to the people around us, we just might be fanning their spiritual lives back into flame. ✳

*So accept each other just as Christ has accepted you;
then God will be glorified.* — *Romans 15:7* NLT

When my kids were small, I cared a little too much about what image they were presenting to the watching world. I made sure that our little girls had their matching outfits and big bows and little smocked dresses that seemed to be the expected norm in our circle of friends. Everyone looked at us as the "star's family," seeing if we were coiffed and dressed in the latest fashion. Subconsciously, I think I wanted people to look at Mattie and think, *Oh, look, Mattie's perfect, just like Denise, and Denise is such a good mother!*

Mattie was not particularly helpful with this little illusion. She hated ribbons and frills. She'd grab hold of the cute bow in her shiny hair, throw it down on the ground, and be happy as could be. Just like me when I was little—as my daddy had reminded me so often over the years—she wanted to be a boy. She had a boy's bowl haircut, and only wanted to wear boy tennis shoes, jeans, and baggy shirts. She did not want dolls. She did not want tiny monogrammed purses. If I tried to accessorize her, she'd sneak away and take off the cute little pink outfits and put on boyish clothes that didn't match.

I THINK I WANTED PEOPLE TO LOOK AT MATTIE AND THINK, *OH, LOOK, MATTIE'S PERFECT, JUST LIKE DENISE.*

At the time, I was so insecure that I thought people would see mismatched Mattie and think I was a bad mother. Now, though, whenever I see a child wearing strange clothes that don't go together, I don't think that she has a bad mother. No, I think she's got a mother with a healthy enough sense of self-confidence that she can let her child dress herself. That mom is not hyper-concerned about what other people might think. ✳

I have loved you with an everlasting love;
Therefore with lovingkindness I have drawn you.
— *Jeremiah 31:3*

Early in Alan's career, we had agreed that my being home with our girls would help create a more "normal" childhood for them. Although that was wonderful, it wasn't always tremendously stimulating. Like many stay-at-home mothers, on many nights I'd think back over the hours and wonder, *What did I really accomplish today?* I had done important things, for sure, but sometimes I felt that I didn't have a whole lot of purpose or worth in other people's eyes.

Meanwhile, Alan was growing professionally, constantly making new music, thriving in his songwriting and singing life, and receiving plenty of praise and accolades. As he was growing in his work and getting lots of personal affirmation, I felt as if I was shrinking. After all, most of my identity was rooted in pretty superficial things: how I looked and what people thought of me. I didn't have the deep roots of security that come from knowing real significance in a personal relationship with God.

And since I'd drifted from faith over the years, the only anchor in my life was Alan. Tethered to him, I had a sense of who I was. By his side, I was a woman to be envied.

HE HAD BECOME MY FOUNDATION. SO WHEN HE LEFT, THERE WAS NOTHING LEFT FOR ME TO DEPEND ON.

Over the years, he had become my foundation. So when he left, there was nothing left for me to depend on. My house had been built on shifting sands, and now in the storms of fear, anger, pain, and confusion, I felt as if everything was going to collapse.

By the grace of God, I started taking baby steps toward a new way of thinking that eventually led to a new kind of happiness. I already knew that no amount of material stuff could bring contentment. And I was realizing, too, that no human relationship—even if it seems "perfect"—can really satisfy the deepest longings of a person's soul. The devastation of Alan's departure was leading me to a new beginning, new freedom, and the utter security of a new love I had looked for all my life. ✸

God soon turns from His wrath, but he never turns from His love. —Charles Haddon Spurgeon

ONLY GOD CAN FILL
OUR LONGING TO BE LOVED AND
ACCEPTED, OUR LONGING TO BELONG.
HIS LOVE, MORE THAN ANY
HUMAN LOVE, MAKES US WHOLE.

We know what real love is because Christ gave up his life for us. And so we also ought to give up our lives for our Christian brothers and sisters. —1 John 3:16 NLT

I'm not sure the women in my weekly Bible study will ever fully realize the impact they had on my life during such a trying time.

Jane was our organizer. Raised in Memphis, she was (and is) the epitome of Southern graciousness. We'd sit in a circle in her cozy family room, some of us dressed for the day and others in sweats and no makeup. The casualness and security came from the long-standing bond that we had with one another.

I BECAME MORE AND MORE FREE TO BE THE REAL ME—EVEN AS I WAS DISCOVERING WHO THE REAL ME REALLY WAS!

Each week our group would dig into different sections of the Bible. We'd talk about our struggles, and then we'd sit in that circle, hold hands, and pray.

I had been spiritually dry for so long that I was dying for truth. I was so thirsty and hungry for God, and I could taste His presence in this little circle of women who loved Him too. So I became more and more free to be the real me—even as I was discovering who the real me really was!

But this wasn't just a support group, as wonderful as such groups can be. Most important, the women there shared a common commitment to God. They knew He was the only One who could truly help any of us, because only God has the supernatural power to change us. We weren't just focused on one another; we were all focused on Him, and as we learned more about Him and drew closer to Him, we drew closer to one another as well.

These sisters were rock-solid there for me. They loved me, cried and laughed with me, and pleaded with God to restore my marriage and shower His love on me. Their love taught me about God's love and how to be real with Him and with myself. And that was a priceless lesson that came at just the right time. ✵

You will keep him in perfect peace,
whose mind is stayed on You,
because he trusts in You. — *Isaiah 26:3*

When Alan left, people gave me plenty of advice. "Get the best lawyer money can buy, and take Alan for everything you can get." And "Make sure he sees you with someone else." They meant well, but besides talking as if we were back in high school or something, these people's bits of advice were actually pretty unhealthy. Fueled by rage, they were all about retribution and gain.

Not that I didn't consider them all at some point! Anger came quite naturally to me. At one point I threw all of Alan's remaining clothes into the back of a pickup truck so a friend could dump them at his rental home. If he was not going to live with me, then I could at least have more closet space.

But as time went by, a miracle happened. I found myself drawn by God's Spirit into a different response altogether. It wasn't me, as if I became a great heroine who was far above normal human reactions, Saint Denise of Nashville.

No, I just found that the more I pursued my new relationship with Jesus and the more I explored the Bible, the more my attitudes were changing. It was incredible.

Instead of my thoughts running like a gerbil on a wheel when I went to bed at night, I'd pray out loud. I'd proclaim God's promises for His peace and His love to my empty bedroom. After all, it wasn't like I was keeping Alan awake; he wasn't there. But I wasn't alone. God was with me. I could go to sleep in peace as I grabbed hold of His truths in my mind and meditated on them in my heart.

THE MORE I PURSUED MY NEW RELATIONSHIP WITH JESUS, THE MORE MY ATTITUDES WERE CHANGING.

Drawing my nourishment from the Bible and sustained by God's love, I was growing stronger in the perspective of what really mattered. Faith. Hope. Love. ✺

Yes, God's grace is always sufficient,
and His arms are always open to give it.
But, will our arms be open to receive it?
— Beth Moore

JESUS TEACHES
US THAT THOSE WHO
HAVE BEEN FORGIVEN MUCH
HAVE GREAT LOVE FOR
THE ONE WHO FORGIVES THEM.
WHEN WE ACKNOWLEDGE
OUR SINS BEFORE HIM, WE RECEIVE
HIS AMAZING LOVE AND FORGIVENESS,
AND OUR LOVE FOR HIM GROWS
EVER STRONGER.

Bear with each other and forgive whatever grievances you may have against one another. Forgive as the Lord forgave you.
—*Colossians 3:13* NIV

In order for Alan and me to have a truly fresh start, we had to rebuild trust. The deepest wound had been the destruction of trust because of betrayal in our relationship. Alan had not been faithful. And he had covered it up.

It felt so strange and awful. On one hand he was so familiar to me, the man he'd always been . . . but on the other hand he seemed to be a different person altogether. I would look at his face, his eyes, his hands, and think, *How could the man I'd known and loved all these years, with whom I'd had three children, have had this hidden part of his life I knew nothing about?* I was so full of anger, shame, and pain that I hardly knew which way to turn.

But God had entered into this sad story. He had brought me a long way. He was working in Alan as well, bringing him back to Himself and also to me.

I was thankful, in a really painful way, that Alan had brought it all out in the open. I appreciated that he was courageous enough to tell all and ask for my pardon. After all, if he wasn't repentant, we weren't going to get anywhere in rebuilding our relationship.

I WAS SO FULL OF ANGER, SHAME, AND PAIN THAT I HARDLY KNEW WHICH WAY TO TURN.

But the first step lay with me, and it was a huge challenge. Would I really forgive? Could I forgive? Or would I smooth things over in a superficial way, taking Alan back and acting as if all was well, but still holding on to his wrongs like aces up my sleeve, cards to be whipped out whenever I needed to trump him?

My lifelong habit of denial was not going to work in this situation. I couldn't just cover things over and forge ahead, acting as if nothing had happened. In order for me—as well as Alan—to be set free, I had to clearly acknowledge the wrongs he'd done. And then if we wanted to go forward, I had to forgive. There was no escaping it.

In the long run, I found that forgiveness unlocked all kinds of new blessings. But of course when I found myself confronted with the need to forgive Alan, I couldn't see ahead to the good things that forgiveness would bring in my future. All I knew was that if I was really going to do everything that I could do to make my marriage work, I had to forgive Alan completely. I felt anxious and pained by the whole process, but I also felt a strong sense of God's presence. I really knew He is always faithful, even if human beings aren't.

I prayed, pouring out my concerns to God. I asked Him to do things in my heart that I just could not do on my own. I asked Him to erase pictures in my mind that had tortured me. I asked Him to free me from rage. And I prayed that He would help me to be the loving, forgiving wife that I wanted to be.

I KNEW THAT IF I WAS REALLY GOING TO DO EVERYTHING THAT I COULD DO TO MAKE MY MARRIAGE WORK, I HAD TO FORGIVE ALAN COMPLETELY.

I knew I could not be that person through my own good intentions or willpower. I wasn't strong enough. But God was strong enough to do miracles in me, starting with giving me His peace right in the midst of the pain of Alan's betrayal. And God kept the miracles coming, giving me what I needed to be able to forgive my husband. ✺

When you forgive, you in no way change the past—
but you sure do change the future.
— Bernard Meltzer

THERE'S NO ONE-SIZE-FITS-ALL
FORMULA FOR FORGIVENESS.
FOR EACH OF US, THE
STRUGGLE WILL BE INDIVIDUAL.
BUT I'VE FOUND THAT FORGIVENESS
IS THE KEY TO REAL FREEDOM IN LIFE.
IT FREES US FROM THE BITTERNESS
AND RESENTMENT THAT MIGHT
OTHERWISE DESTROY US.

And be kind to one another,
tenderhearted, forgiving one another, even as
God in Christ forgave you. — *Ephesians 4:32*

As Alan and I made our way through the tender time of rebuilding our marriage, we really believed that our slates had been wiped clean, that God had given us a fresh start. But we've also had to keep working at certain principles. We've had to realize and practice the truth that real biblical forgiveness is an ongoing, daily process. As long as we live, we will have to face the reality of our dark side, what the Bible calls our sin nature.

I've realized this more and more in my daily prayer time. The Bible says, "If we claim to be without sin, we deceive ourselves and the truth is not in us. If we confess our sins, he is faithful and just and will forgive us our sins and purify us from all unrighteousness" (1 John 1:8–10 NIV).

When I'm sitting with my prayer journal in the morning, I've found it really helpful to write down anything from the previous day that I need forgiveness for. God will often prompt me to remember something that I hadn't even been thinking about: talking impatiently with someone, not spending time with one of our girls when she needed me . . . the list goes on and on.

HE LOVES ME, AND AS I CONFESS MY SINS AND SHORTCOMINGS, HE FORGIVES THEM FREELY AND RESTORES OUR RELATIONSHIP.

But each day I know that God hears my prayers! He knows my heart. He's changing me, day by day. He loves me, and as I confess my sins and shortcomings, He forgives them freely and restores our relationship.

Incredible!

Though Alan and I are obviously both sinful humans, the same principle applies in our relationship. We try to address hurts and misunderstandings every day as they occur, so that they don't drive a wedge between us. This practice just follows the basic principle our mothers always told us when we were growing up: you have to take the trash out every single day . . . or it starts to stink. ✳

Therefore bear fruits worthy of repentance.
—Matthew 3:8

My forgiveness of Alan's infidelity didn't mean that I was blind or had stuck my head in the sand. As we moved forward, I didn't just want nice words. I wanted to see different actions, so I could reasonably expect different outcomes.

Thankfully, Alan not only told me that he wanted to save and restore our marriage. He showed me, in tangible ways, by humbly doing whatever he could to demonstrate that he was willing to live transparently. No secrets.

For one thing, Alan was very sensitive to how I was feeling. As I worked through everything going on inside of me, I had a lot of anger, tears, and frustration. He would not only let me vent, but he also really heard my pain. He tried to understand and empathize with the thunderstorm of emotions that was flooding the dry ground inside me.

Alan also made changes in his professional life. To avoid the temptations that can come with life on the road, he started flying to every engagement rather than taking the tour bus. He called me and our children all the time, giving us short accounts of where he was and what he was doing. There was never a time when I couldn't get him to answer his cell phone when I called, as there had been before. And almost without exception, he flew home after every show rather than staying out on the road. He broke off relationships with people whose influence might negatively affect his new commitment.

No one is perfect. But as much as Alan's unfaithfulness had hurt me, his willingness to change his behaviors and work hard to make a new start impressed me.

AS MUCH AS ALAN'S UNFAITHFULNESS HAD HURT ME, HIS WILLINGNESS TO CHANGE HIS BEHAVIORS AND WORK HARD TO MAKE A NEW START IMPRESSED ME.

Real repentance is freeing; it lifts the burden of guilt. And true repentance is shown not just by words, but by deeds. When we repent with our actions as well as with our words, we make room for God's precious restoration work in our lives. ✸

Be devoted to one another in brotherly love.
Honor one another above yourselves. Never be lacking in zeal,
but keep your spiritual fervor, serving the Lord.
— Romans 12:10–11 NIV

On a crisp fall evening last year, Alan and I stood at the edge of the football field at our daughters' high school, feeling as if we were about eighty years old. It was Mattie's homecoming game, and her classmates had elected her as a member of the homecoming court.

At halftime, we climbed down from the stands and stood in front of the chain-link fence adjacent to the field. When the announcer called Mattie's name, Alan and I whooped, clapped, and took several million pictures as Mattie and her escort, Michael, took their places in a semicircle with the rest of the homecoming court.

As I watched Mattie with her long, coral dress and her dark hair gleaming in the lights of the football stadium, I was suddenly struck by a sense of déjà vu, or time travel, or both. I remembered so clearly when I was Mattie's age, standing in the bright lights, my whole life in front of me. Alan had been my escort all those years ago . . . and now here we were, hanging on the stadium fence while our daughter experienced her own high school rite of passage.

As I looked up at Alan and back at Mattie, I thought how very strange life is. No matter how much we romanticize relationships, fulfillment, and the future when we're teenagers, real love stories play out much longer, and with a lot more complexity, than a two-and-a-half-minute song on the radio.

In real life the prince and princess don't just put on the glass slipper, or get rid of the evil stepmother or the villain, and then it's happily ever after. As Alan's very first #1 record put it, "The boy don't always get the girl / here in the real world."

REAL LOVE STORIES PLAY OUT MUCH LONGER, AND WITH A LOT MORE COMPLEXITY, THAN A TWO-AND-A-HALF-MINUTE SONG ON THE RADIO.

In real life, heroes and heroines go through all kinds of struggles, trouble, and heartaches. If they don't die young, they get wrinkles and lose their hair. They laugh and cry together through many decades.

They break each other's hearts and help each other heal. Real love matures. It means having to say you're sorry. Real love is deeper, wilder, and stronger than the two-hour romances we see at the movies.

I'm just beginning to learn about that kind of real love. I haven't figured it all out, and even if I had, I still wouldn't be able to live it day in and day out. I practice "real love" imperfectly at best.

I DON'T HAVE TO BE PERFECT. I CAN'T BE PERFECT. BUT I KNOW THAT HE IS WITH ME, FORGIVING ME WHEN I FAIL AND PICKING ME UP WHEN I FALL.

But that's where I find *real* life in my relationship with Jesus—it's so absolutely freeing. I don't have to be perfect. I can't be perfect. But I know that He is with me, forgiving me when I fail and picking me up when I fall. And because of His presence and power with me, I can begin to be the wife, mother, daughter, and friend that He designed me to be. �֍

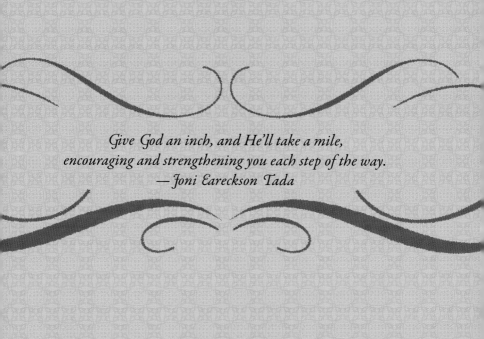

Give God an inch, and He'll take a mile,
encouraging and strengthening you each step of the way.
— *Joni Eareckson Tada*

WHEN WE TAKE STEPS OF OBEDIENCE,
GOD USES OUR EFFORTS TO DO
HIS WORK IN OUR LIVES
AND IN THE LIVES OF OTHERS.
THE REWARD FOR FOLLOWING HIM
IS A LIFETIME OF UNEXPECTED
BLESSINGS AND REDEMPTION.

AFTERWORD:
GOD'S ROAD HOME

When God leads us home, we experience new joy and purpose.
We see our past redeemed and restored. We see old wounds
healed and even our gravest mistakes transformed
into a tool for God's glory.

I'm no theologian, but I do know what I know. I'm like the blind man Jesus healed in the gospel of John. When he was questioned as to exactly why this miracle had happened, he said, "I don't know!" Then he went on, "One thing I do know. Once I was blind, but now I see!"

That's a little like my story in this book. One thing I do know: even though I had all the material things we chase after in this world, I once was miserable, full of uncertainty and fear. But now I have real joy and peace! God has led me home to His wonderful love, and now I know firsthand that a life lived in the sweet riches of God's amazing grace is far better than any earthly comfort.

God promises us that all we have to do to find our way home is trust Him with our lives, to give Him the steering wheel. He is there, waiting for us to turn our eyes to Him. When we do, we find that He has a better story written for us than any so-called fairy tale we could ever imagine. ❀

This life of faith, then, consists just in this—
being a child in the Father's house.
Let the ways of childish confidence and freedom from care,
which so please you and win your heart when you observe your
own little ones, teach you what you should be
in your attitude toward God.
—Hannah Whitall Smith